William Joyce's
Mother Goose

Random House 🏠 New York

Old King Cole
Was a merry old soul,
And a merry old soul was he;
He called for his pipe,
And he called for his bowl,
And he called for his fiddlers three.

Every fiddler he had a fiddle,
And a very fine fiddle had he;
Oh, there's none so rare
As can compare
With King Cole and his fiddlers three.

As I went to Bonner
I met a pig
Without a wig,
Upon my word and honor.

Yankee Doodle came to town,
　Riding on a pony;
He stuck a feather in his hat
And called it macaroni.

Pussy cat, pussy cat,
　Where have you been?
I've been to London
　To look at the Queen.
Pussy cat, pussy cat,
　What did you do there?
I frightened a little mouse
　Under her chair.

Humpty Dumpty sat on a wall.
Humpty Dumpty had a great fall;

All the king's horses and all the king's men
Couldn't put Humpty together again.

Wee Willie Winkie runs through the town,
Upstairs and downstairs, in his nightgown;
Tapping at the window, crying at the lock:
"Are the babes in their beds, for it's now ten o'clock?"

There was an old woman who lived in a shoe,
    She had so many children she didn't know what to do;
She gave them some broth, without any bread,
    And whipped them all soundly, and sent them to bed.

Sing a song of sixpence, a pocket full of rye,
Four and twenty blackbirds baked in a pie;
When the pie was opened the birds began to sing,
And wasn't this a dainty dish to set before the king?

Mary, Mary, quite contrary,
How does your garden grow?
With silver bells and cockleshells
And pretty maids all in a row.

Pat-a-cake, pat-a-cake, Baker's man,
Bake me a cake as fast as you can.
Pat it and prick it and mark it with B,
Put it in the oven for baby and me.

Little Miss Muffet
Sat on a tuffet,
    Eating her curds and whey;

There came a great spider,
Who sat down beside her,
    And frightened Miss Muffet away.

Hickery, dickery, dock,
The mouse ran up the clock;

The clock struck one,
The mouse ran down,
Hickery, dickery, dock.

Hey diddle diddle,
The cat and the fiddle,
The cow jumped over the moon.
The little dog laughed
To see such sport,
And the dish ran away with the spoon.

Rock-a-bye, baby, on the treetop,
When the wind blows the cradle will rock;
When the bough breaks the cradle will fall,
Down will come baby, cradle, and all.

Little Boy Blue,
    Come blow your horn,
The sheep's in the meadow,
    The cow's in the corn.
Where's the little boy
    Who looks after the sheep?
Under the haystack,
    Fast asleep.
Will you wake him?
    No, not I.
For if I do,
    He's sure to cry.

Jack and Jill went up the hill,
To fetch a pail of water;
Jack fell down, and broke his crown,
And Jill came tumbling after.

Little Tommy Tittlemouse
Lived in a little house;
He caught fishes
In other men's ditches.

Mary had a little lamb,
Its fleece was white as snow;
And everywhere that Mary went
The lamb was sure to go.
It followed her to school one day,
That was against the rule;
It made the children laugh and play
To see a lamb at school.

Jack Sprat could eat no fat.
His wife could eat no lean;
And so between them both, you see,
They licked the platter clean.

There was a little girl, and she had a little curl
Right in the middle of her forehead;
When she was good, she was very, very good,
But when she was bad, she was horrid.

Little Jack Horner
Sat in the corner,
Eating a Christmas pie.
He put in his thumb,
And pulled out a plum,
And said, "What a good boy am I!"

Old Mother Hubbard
Went to the cupboard
To fetch her poor dog a bone;
But when she got there
The cupboard was bare,
And so the poor dog had none.

Old Mother Goose
    When she wanted to wander,
Would ride through the air
    On a very fine gander.

Three blind mice, see how they run!
They all ran after the farmer's wife,
Who cut off their tails with a carving knife,
Did you ever see such a thing in your life
As three blind mice?

Peter, Peter, pumpkin eater,
Had a wife and couldn't keep her;
He put her in a pumpkin shell,
And there he kept her very well.

Georgie Porgie, pudding and pie,
Kissed the girls and made them cry;
When the boys came out to play,
Georgie Porgie ran away.

Rub-a-dub-dub,
Three men in a tub;
And who do you think they be?
The butcher, the baker,
The candlestick-maker;
They all jumped out of a rotten potato,
Turn 'em out, knaves all three!

Twinkle, twinkle, little star,
How I wonder what you are!
Up above the world so high,
Like a diamond in the sky.

Diddle, diddle, dumpling, my son John,
Went to bed with his breeches on,
One stocking off, and one stocking on,
Diddle, diddle, dumpling, my son John.

Hark, hark,
The dogs do bark,
The beggars are coming to town;
Some in rags,
And some in tags,
And one in a velvet gown.